3523
© 1995 by Coombe Books
ISBN 1-85833-258-3

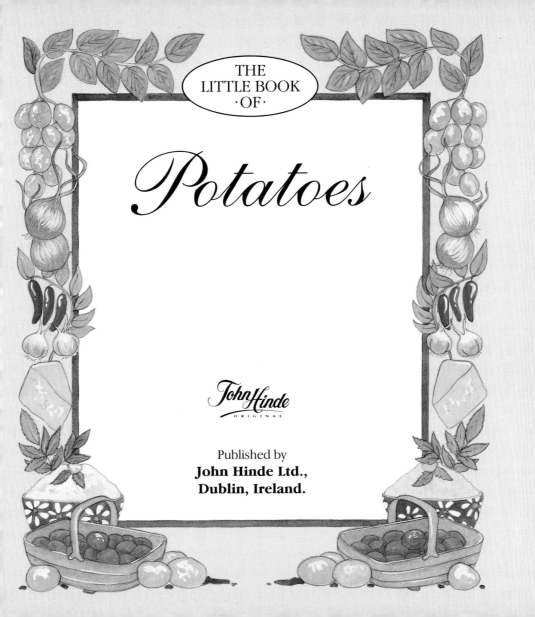

THE LITTLE BOOK ·OF·

Potatoes

John Hinde
ORIGINAL

Published by
**John Hinde Ltd.,
Dublin, Ireland.**

Introduction

Native to South America, the potato was encountered there by the Spanish invaders and subsequently introduced into Europe in the 16th century. At first, being new and scarce, they were food only for the rich. By the 19th century, however, they became widely available, and indeed the poorer people ate little else, to the extent that when potato blight hit Ireland from 1845 to 1851, the resultant famine caused the death of over a million Irish people.

There are dozens of different varieties of potato, each with its own characteristics. There are subtle taste variations between types, and significant differences in texture, ranging from the firm-fleshed, waxy varieties, such as the Maine, which are so delicious when boiled with a sprig of mint and served hot with butter or cold in salads, to the disintegrating, mealy types, such as the Russet, which are perfect for baking, mashing and pureeing.

For flavor, there is nothing to compare **with** new potatoes. These are dug in early spring, while still **small** and sweet, and they have a high vitamin C content. They should be eaten fresh, and not stored for longer than 48 hours, after which their texture and flavor tend to deteriorate. Their skins are damp and rub off easily, and they need only to be scrubbed clean before being cooked. They are at their best just boiled.

Mature potatoes are harvested from September to October, once their green tops have died and their sugar content has been converted into starch. Stored in a cool, dry, dark place, they will keep well for several weeks, or even months.

Some people like to peel their potatoes, while others love the flavor and "bite" of the skins left on. If you peel them, then do so thinly, as much of the goodness and the vitamins lie just beneath the skin.

It is hard to think of a cooking method that cannot be used for the preparation of potatoes. We boil them, fry them, bake them, steam them, mash them and curry them. The advent of the microwave oven has greatly popularized the baked potato as a quick and nourishing lunch or supper dish. Potatoes are easy to grow, and even improve the soil. They are cheap to buy, and wonderfully filling – in short, the potato is a most obliging, versatile and popular food.

Potatoes are not eaten raw and are rarely used in desserts, but otherwise there are endless possibilities for this humble but incredibly versatile vegetable. It thickens soups, fills pancakes, deliciously absorbs flavors in curries and stews, and can be whipped, chipped and fashioned into any number of attractive shapes. Glance through the imaginative recipes in these pages to discover something of the potato's tremendous culinary potential.

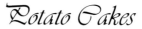

Potato Cakes

SERVES 6-8

These fried potato cakes make a delicious snack or side-dish.

PREPARATION: 15 mins
COOKING: 6 mins

1 cup all-purpose flour
½ tsp salt
½ tsp baking powder
2 tbsps butter
4 cups mashed potato
Bacon grease or oil

1. Sift the flour, salt, and baking powder into a mixing bowl. Rub in the butter until evenly blended.

2. Mix in the mashed potatoes and knead the mixture into a ball.

3. Cut the potato mixture in half and roll out each half, on a floured board or work surface, into a circle about ½ inch thick. Divide each circle into four segments.

4. Heat a griddle or heavy-based skillet until very hot. Add a little bacon grease or oil to the pan and slide in some of the potato cakes. Cook 2-3 minutes on each side until hot and browned.

Potato Soup

SERVES 8-10

Potatoes make a tasty and hearty soup which requires no thickening.

PREPARATION: 15 mins
COOKING: 1 hr

2 pounds potatoes
2 medium onions
1 small carrot
4 tbsps butter
5 cups broth
2½ cups milk
Bayleaf, thyme and parsley
Salt and pepper
Cream and chives, for garnish

1. Peel and slice the potatoes, onions, and carrot. Melt butter in a large saucepan and sauté the onions in it until soft but not brown.

2. Add the potatoes and carrot. Stir in the broth and milk.

3. Tie the bayleaf, thyme, and parsley together, and add to the pan, along with salt and pepper to taste.

4. Simmer gently about 1 hour, remove herbs and blend or put through a sieve or vegetable mill.

5. Add some cream before serving, and sprinkle with chopped chives.

Potatoes with Garlic and Chilies

SERVES 4-6

These are rather like spicy French fries, but they are not deep-fried.

PREPARATION: 15-20 mins
COOKING: 15 mins

---

1 pound potatoes, peeled and washed
3 tbsps cooking oil
½ tsp black mustard seeds
½ tsp cumin seeds
4 cloves garlic, crushed
¼-½ tsp chili powder
½ tsp ground turmeric
1 tsp salt or to taste

---

1. Cut the potatoes to the thickness of French fries, but half their normal length.

2. In a large nonstick or cast iron skillet, heat the oil over a medium heat.

3. Add the mustard seeds and then the cumin. When the seeds start popping, add the garlic and allow it to lightly brown.

4. Remove the pan from the heat and stir in the chili powder and turmeric.

5. Add the potatoes and place the pan back on the heat. Stir, and increase the heat to medium.

6. Add the salt, stir and mix, then cover the pan and cook 3-4 minutes, and stir again. Continue to do this until the potatoes are cooked through and lightly browned. Remove from the heat.

Pommes Dauphiné

SERVES 6

This dish from the mountainous province of France is robust fare.

PREPARATION: 25 mins
COOKING: 30-40 mins

1 clove garlic, crushed
2 tbsps butter
4½ cups potatoes, peeled and thinly sliced
¾ cup grated yellow cheese
Salt and pepper
6 tbsps butter cut into very small dice
⅔ cup half-and-half

1. Rub the bottom and sides of a heavy baking dish with the crushed clove of garlic. Grease the bottom and sides liberally with butter.

2. Spread half of the potato slices in the bottom of the dish, sprinkle with half of the cheese, some salt and pepper, and dot with half the butter. Top with the remaining slices of potato, neatly arranged. Sprinkle with the

Step 2 Layer the potatoes with the cheese and seasoning.

remaining cheese, salt and pepper, and butter.

3. Pour the cream down the inside of the dish around the potatoes.

4. Cook in the top part of an oven preheated to 400°F, 30-40 minutes, or until the potatoes are tender and the top is nicely browned. Serve immediately.

Step 1 Rub the dish with garlic, and butter it well.

Step 3 Pour in the cream down the inside of the dish.

Hot Potato Salad with Bacon

SERVES 6-8

If Germany has a national salad this must be it. It is perfect with any of the country's many varieties of sausage.

PREPARATION: 25 mins
COOKING: 35 mins

6-8 even-sized waxy potatoes
Pinch salt
4 slices Canadian bacon, diced
1 onion
⅔ cup white wine vinegar
⅔ cup water or beef broth
3 tbsps sour cream (optional)
Salt and pepper
2 tbsps chopped parsley

---

1. Boil the potatoes in their skins in lightly-salted water to cover. When they are just tender,

Step 2 Follow the natural lines in the onion and make vertical cuts through the onion nearly to the root end.

Step 2 Cut the onion crosswise before mincing.

drain, and peel while still hot. Cut into thin slices and place in a serving dish.

2. Fry the bacon in a large skillet. Meanwhile, mince the onion. Once the bacon is pale golden, add the onion and continue to sauté slowly, until transparent but not brown.

3. Remove the pan from the heat, and gradually pour in the vinegar and the water or broth. Bring to the boil and remove from the heat.

4. Stir in the sour cream, if using, and pour the mixture over the potatoes. Lift the potatoes so that the dressing runs over them evenly. Sprinkle with salt, pepper, and parsley. Serve immediately.

Pommes Noisettes

SERVES 4-6

These delicious cheesy potato balls will complement any meal, from a sophisticated dinner party to a family get-together.

PREPARATION: 15 mins, plus chilling
COOKING: 30 mins

---

4 cups potatoes, peeled and cut into chunks
2 tbsps butter or margarine
Salt and freshly ground black pepper
4 tbsps yellow cheese, finely grated
4 tbsps ground hazelnuts or almonds
Oil for shallow frying
Fresh parsley or watercress sprigs, to garnish

---

1. Cook the potatoes in boiling salted water until tender, then drain and mash well.

2. Add the butter or margarine, seasoning, and cheese and fork through until well combined, then refrigerate until completely cold.

3. Shape spoonfuls of the cold mashed potato into 1-inch balls.

Step 4 Shape spoonfuls of the refrigerated mashed potato into balls approximately 1 inch in diameter.

4. Spread the nuts on a plate and roll the potato balls in the nuts, making sure they are well-coated.

5. Heat the oil in a large skillet and sauté the potato balls until golden, turning frequently until they are lightly browned and crisp.

6. Serve garnished with parsley or watercress.

Aloo Ki Bhaji

SERVES 4-6

Boiled potatoes, diced, and braised with a few whole spices and onions make a quick and easy side-dish.

PREPARATION: 35-45 mins
COOKING: 20 mins

1½ pounds potatoes
5-6 tbsps cooking oil
½ tsp black mustard seeds
2-3 dried red chilies
⅛ tsp fenugreek (methi) seeds
2 large onions, finely sliced
1-2 fresh green chilies, sliced lengthwise, seeded if wished
1 tsp ground turmeric
1 tsp salt or to taste
2 tbsps chopped coriander (cilantro) leaves

---

1. Boil the potatoes in their skins and allow to cool thoroughly.

2. Peel the potatoes and dice them evenly.

3. Heat the oil in a large skillet over medium heat, add the mustard seeds and sauté until they pop.

4. Add the dried red chilies and the fenugreek seeds, then immediately follow with the onions and the fresh green chilies.

5. Fry the onions 8-10 minutes, or until they are golden-brown.

6. Add the turmeric, potatoes, and salt. Stir and sauté gently another 8-10 minutes, or until the potatoes are heated through.

7. Remove from heat and stir in the coriander (cilantro) leaves.

Potato Whip

SERVES 4

This is an excellent way of using up leftover mashed potatoes, and making them taste just as good, if not better than when they were first cooked!

PREPARATION: 10 mins
COOKING: 30 mins

2 tbsps butter or margarine
6 cups cold mashed potatoes
4 tbsps hot milk
2 eggs, separated
Freshly grated nutmeg
Salt and pepper
4 tbsps grated yellow cheese

1. Melt the butter and beat it into the cold mashed potatoes together with the hot milk and egg yolks. Season well with the nutmeg, salt, and pepper.

2. Whisk the egg whites until stiff and fold them gently but thoroughly into the potato mixture.

3. Pile the mixture into a baking dish and smooth the top level. Sprinkle with the grated cheese and bake in an oven preheated to 400°F about 30 minutes, or until the cheese topping is nicely browned, and the potato mixture piping hot.

Potato and Chestnut Hot-pot

SERVES 4-6

This enticing stew is ideal for a vegetarian meal if served with a lightly-cooked green vegetable.

PREPARATION: 20 mins
COOKING: 1¼ hrs

1½ pounds potatoes
3 medium onions
1 cup brown lentils
2 cups fresh chestnuts, shelled and peeled
Salt and pepper
2 cups warm broth
4 tbsps butter or margarine

---

1. Peel and slice the potatoes and onions thinly.

2. Put layers of potatoes, onions, lentils, and chestnuts into a greased pie pan ending with a layer of potatoes.

3. Season well between each layer and pour the warm broth over the dish.

4. Dot with margarine and cover. Bake in an oven preheated to 375°F for 1 hour, or until the potatoes are tender.

5. Increase the oven temperature to 400°F, remove the lid from the casserole, and return to the oven for 10-15 minutes or until the potatoes are crispy and golden-brown on top.

Colcannon

SERVES 4

This classic Irish potato dish is wonderful served with boiled ham.

PREPARATION: 10 mins
COOKING: 15 mins

4 tbsps butter
4 minced onions, leeks, or green onions/
    scallions
4 tbsps milk
2 cups cooked mashed potatoes
3 cups cooked cabbage

1. Heat the butter in a pan until foaming. Add the onion, leek, or green onions (scallions) and sauté until soft.

2. Add the milk and the well-mashed potatoes and stir until heated through.

3. Chop the cabbage finely and beat into the mixture over a low heat until all the mixture is pale green and fluffy.

Nutty Potato Patties

MAKES 8 CAKES

Serve these delicious patties with broiled meat or fish and salad.

PREPARATION: 10 mins
COOKING: 25 mins

---

1 pound potatoes
1 tbsp butter or margarine
A little milk
6 tbsps mixed nuts, finely ground
2 tbsps sunflower seeds, finely ground
2 tbsps finely chopped green onions (scallions)
Salt and freshly ground black pepper
Flour for coating
Oil for frying

---

1. Peel the potatoes, cut into pieces, and boil until just soft.

2. Drain and mash with the butter and milk to a creamy consistency.

3. Add the nuts, seeds, green onions (scallions) and salt and pepper to taste.

4. If necessary, add a little more milk at this stage, to give a soft texture which holds together.

5. Divide the mixture into 8 and shape into patties, using wet hands.

6. Coat the cakes with flour, shaking off any excess, and fry quickly in a little oil. Drain on kitchen paper and serve immediately.

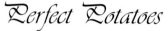

Perfect Potatoes

SERVES 4-6

Potatoes become extra special when teamed up with the flavor of onion.

PREPARATION: 15 mins
COOKING: 1-1½ hrs

---

2 pounds potatoes
1 large onion
Salt and pepper
1¼ cups milk
3 tbsps butter or margarine

---

1. Peel and finely slice the potatoes and onion.

2. Layer the potato slices and onion in a shallow ovenproof dish, sprinkling each layer with some salt and pepper.

3. Pour the milk over them, and dot with the butter or margarine.

4. Bake, uncovered, in an oven preheated to 350°F for 1-1½ hours, or until the potatoes are soft and golden-brown on top.

Bavarian Potato Salad

SERVES 4-6

It is best to prepare this salad a few hours in advance, to allow the potatoes to absorb the flavors. Serve with cold roasts.

PREPARATION: 15 mins
COOKING: 15 mins

---

2 pounds tiny new potatoes
4 tbsps olive oil
4 green onions (scallions), finely chopped
1 clove garlic, crushed
2 tbsps fresh dill, chopped, or 1 tbsp dried dill
2 tbsps wine vinegar
½ tsp sugar
Seasoning
2 tbsps chopped fresh parsley

---

1. Wash the potatoes but do not peel. Put them into a pan, cover with cold water and some salt, and boil until just tender.

2. While the potatoes are cooking, heat the olive oil in a skillet and cook the green onions (scallions) and garlic 2-3 minutes or until they have softened a little.

3. Add the dill and cook gently for a further minute.

4. Add the wine vinegar and sugar, and stir until the sugar dissolves. Remove from the heat and add a little seasoning.

5. Drain the potatoes, and pour the dressing over them whilst they are still hot.

6. Allow to cool and sprinkle with the chopped parsley before serving.

Watercress Potato Skins

SERVES 4

An unusual and tasty way of serving potato skins as an entrée.

PREPARATION: 20 mins
COOKING: 1¼ hours

---

4 large baking potatoes, scrubbed
4 eggs
4 tbsps butter or margarine
1 cup button mushrooms, sliced
1 shallot, peeled and minced
3 tbsps all-purpose flour
2 cups milk
4 tbsps yellow cheese, shredded
Pinch each mustard powder and cayenne
   pepper
Salt and freshly ground black pepper
1 bunch watercress, finely chopped

---

1. Prick the potatoes a few times with a fork and place them directly on the shelf of an oven preheated to 400°F. Bake for ¾-1 hour, depending on the size, or until they are soft when squeezed. Reduce the temperature to 325°F and keep warm while completing the dish.

2. Poach the eggs in gently simmering water for 3½-5 minutes until the white and yolk are just set. Remove from the pan and keep in cold water until required.

3. Melt 1 tbsp of the butter in a small pan and sauté the mushrooms and shallot about 5 minutes or until softened.

4. Melt the remaining butter in a saucepan, stir in the flour, and cook 1 minute. Remove from the heat and gradually stir in 1¼ cups of the milk. Return to the heat and cook gently until thickened. Add the cheese and stir until it melts. Season with the mustard, cayenne, salt, and pepper.

5. Cut a slice off the top of each potato and scoop out the flesh, leaving a border inside each skin to form a firm shell.

6. Put equal amounts of the mushroom mixture into each shell, and top with an egg. Spoon the cheese sauce over the top.

7. Scald the remaining milk, mash the potato flesh, then gradually beat in the hot milk and watercress. Pipe or spoon the potato over the sauce in the potato shell. Sprinkle the top with a little extra cheese and return to the oven for 15 minutes to melt the cheese.

Kashmiri Dum Aloo

SERVES 4

This Indian dish of boiled potatoes fried until golden then simmered in yogurt and spices is a lovely way to serve new potatoes.

PREPARATION: 30-35 mins
COOKING: 20-25 mins

1¼ pounds small new potatoes, scrubbed
2 tbsps ghee or clarified butter
1 tsp fennel seeds

Mix the following 5 ingredients in a small bowl

½ tsp ground cumin
1 tsp ground coriander
¼ tsp freshly ground black pepper
½ tsp ground turmeric
½ tsp ground ginger

⅔ cup thick-set plain yogurt
1 tsp salt or to taste
¼ tsp garam masala or curry powder
1 tbsp chopped coriander (cilantro) leaves
1 fresh green chili, seeded and finely chopped

---

1. Boil the potatoes in their skins, cool, and peel them. Pierce the potatoes all over with a cocktail stick to enable the spices to flavor them thoroughly.

2. Melt the ghee or clarified butter over a medium heat in a nonstick or cast-iron skillet.

3. When the ghee is hot, fry the potatoes in a single layer 8-10 minutes, or until they are browned, turning them frequently. Remove them with a slotted spoon and set aside.

4. Remove the skillet from the heat, and stir in the fennel seeds, followed by the spice mixture. Place the skillet back over a low heat, stir the spices, and sauté 1 minute.

5. Add the yogurt and salt, and mix well. Add the potatoes, cover the skillet, and simmer 10-12 minutes. Stir in the garam masala or curry powder and remove the skillet from the heat.

6. Stir in the coriander (cilantro) leaves and the green chili.

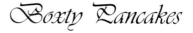

Boxty Pancakes

SERVES 4-6

These Irish pancakes, made from both cooked and raw potatoes, can also be flavored with some chopped herbs, onion, or caraway seeds.

PREPARATION: 15 mins
COOKING: 15 mins

---

8 ounces raw potatoes
8 ounces cooked potatoes, mashed
1 tsp salt
1 tsp baking powder
2 cups all-purpose flour
Pepper
4 tbsps butter, margarine or bacon grease
Milk

---

1. Peel and grate the raw potatoes. Wrap them tightly in a cloth and squeeze over a bowl to extract as much of the starch liquid as possible.

2. Thoroughly blend the grated raw potato into the cooked, mashed potato.

3. Pour the liquid off the bowl of potato starch and scrape the starch into the potato mixture. Sift the salt and baking powder with the flour and add to the potatoes, mixing well.

4. Melt fat, add to the potatoes, and mix again. Add as much milk as necessary to make the mixture into a dough of dropping consistency and season with pepper.

5. Heat some more fat on a griddle or in a heavy-based skillet. When foaming, drop in tablespoons of the mixture.

6. Cook the pancakes in batches for 3-4 minutes on each side or until crispy and golden. Keep warm under a broiler until all are cooked.

Aloo Mattar

SERVES 4-6

This Indian recipe is a semi-moist dish which blends easily with meat, chicken, or fish curries.

PREPARATION: 10-15 mins
COOKING: 25-30 mins

---

4 tbsps cooking oil
1 medium-sized onion, minced
2 cinnamon sticks, broken up
½-inch cube root ginger, peeled and finely chopped
½ tsp ground turmeric
2 tsps ground cumin
¼ tsp chili powder
¼ tsp freshly ground black pepper
1 pound potatoes, peeled and cut into 1-inch cubes
1-2 whole fresh green chilies
1 tbsp tomato paste
1 tsp salt or to taste
1 cup warm water
½ cup frozen garden peas
1 tbsp chopped coriander (cilantro) leaves

1. Heat the oil over a medium heat and sauté the onion, cinnamon, and ginger 4-5 minutes, stirring frequently.

2. Reduce heat to low and add the turmeric, cumin, chili powder, and black pepper. Stir and sauté 1 minute.

3. Add the potatoes and chilies, stir, and cook 2-5 minutes until the spices are blended thoroughly. Stir in the tomato paste and salt.

4. Add the water, bring to the boil, cover the pan, and cook over a medium-to-low heat about 10 minutes or until the potatoes are half-cooked.

5. Add the peas, cover the pan, and cook until the potatoes are tender.

6. Remove the pan from the heat, stir in half the coriander (cilantro) leaves, and sprinkle the remainder on top.

Potato Pierozki

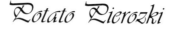

SERVES 6-8

These Polish dumplings are fried and served as a side-dish with meat.

PREPARATION: 30 minutes, plus chilling
COOKING: 8 minutes, per batch

Dough
2 cups all-purpose flour
Pinch salt
⅔ cup butter or margarine
1 egg
1 tbsp sour cream

Filling
2 tbsps butter
1 small onion, minced
1 pound cooked potatoes, mashed
2 egg yolks
Salt and pepper

Oil for frying
Sour cream, to serve

Step 6 Drop the filled and sealed Pierozki into boiling water and cook until they float to the surface.

1. First prepare the Pierozki dough. Sift the flour with a pinch of salt into a large bowl. Cut the butter into small pieces and rub into the flour until the mixture resembles fine breadcrumbs.

2. Mix the egg and sour cream together, and combine with the flour and butter to make a firm dough. Knead the dough together quickly in the bowl, wrap well and chill 30 minutes.

3. To prepare the filling, melt the butter in a small skillet and sauté the onion 3-4 minutes until softened. Combine with the potatoes and egg yolks, and season well.

4. Roll the dough out very thinly on a well-floured surface and cut into circles about 3 inches in diameter.

5. Place teaspoons of the filling onto the dough circles and moisten the edges with water. Fold over the top and seal the edges well, crimping with a fork if wished.

6. To cook the Pierozki, drop a few at a time into boiling water. Simmer 2-3 minutes or until they float to the top. Lift out of the water with a slotted spoon and drain on kitchen paper.

7. When all the Pierozki are done, heat about 4 tbsps oil in a skillet and cook the Pierozki over brisk heat about 3-4 minutes, or until lightly browned on both sides. Place the Pierozki on a serving platter and top with sour cream.